Carols to Sing, Clap and Play

A companion to the descant recorder tuition books by
Heather Cox and Garth Rickard
Designed and illustrated by David Woodroffe

Contents

Nelson

Away in a Manger

1. Away in a manger, no crib for a bed,
   The little Lord Jesus laid down His sweet head,
   The stars in the bright sky looked down where He lay,
   The little Lord Jesus asleep on the hay.

2. The cattle are lowing, the baby awakes,
   But little Lord Jesus, no crying He makes,
   I love Thee, Lord Jesus. Look down from the sky
   And stay by my side until morning is nigh.

3. Be near me, Lord Jesus, I ask Thee to stay
   Close by me for ever, and love me, I pray.
   Bless all the dear children in Thy tender care,
   And fit us for Heaven to live with Thee there.

The tune for this carol is from America.
William James Kirkpatrick, an American born in 1838,
composed it for a Sunday School class.

Recorder 1

Recorder 2

Tuned Percussion
or Recorder 3

Deck the Hall

1. Deck the hall with boughs of holly,
   Fa la la la la, la la la la.
   'Tis the season to be jolly,
   Fa la la la la, la la la la.
   Fill the mead cup, drain the barrel,
   Fa la la, la la la, la la la.
   Troll the ancient Christmas carol,
   Fa la la la la, la la la la.

2. See the flowing bowl before us,
   Strike the harp and join the chorus.
   Follow me in merry measure,
   While I sing of beauty's treasure.

3. Fast away the old year passes,
   Hail the new, ye lads and lasses.
   Laughing, quaffing all together,
   Heedless of the wind and weather.

This is a secular, or non-religious, carol. The tune is
Welsh, and has been sung and danced to for hundreds
of years.

Gabriel's Message

1. The angel Gabriel from heaven came,
   His wings as drifted snow, his eyes as flame,
   "All hail," said he, "thou lowly maiden Mary,
   Most highly favoured lady,"
   Gloria!

2. "For known a blessed Mother thou shalt be,
   All generations laud and honour thee.
   Thy Son shall be Emmanuel, by seers foretold."
   Most highly favoured lady,
   Gloria!

3. Then gentle Mary meekly bowed her head,
   "To me be as it pleaseth God," she said,
   "My soul shall laud and magnify His Holy Name."
   Most highly favoured lady,
   Gloria!

4. Of her, Emmanuel, the Christ, was born
   In Bethlehem, all on a Christmas morn.
   And Christian folk throughout the world will ever say:
   "Most highly favoured lady,
   Gloria!"

As far as we can tell, this very old melody was first sung in a part of France, very near to Spain, known as the Basque region.

*The slur does not apply to the recorder parts.

Hark! The Herald Angels

1. Hark! the herald angels sing,
   "Glory to the new-born King.
   Peace on earth and mercy mild,
   God and sinners reconciled."
   Joyful, all ye nations, rise,
   Join the triumph of the skies,
   With the angelic host proclaim
   "Christ is born in Bethlehem."

   Hark! the herald angels sing
   "Glory to the new-born King."

2. Hail the heaven-born Prince of Peace,
   Hail the Sun of Righteousness.
   Light and life to all He brings,
   Risen with healing in His wings.
   Mild He lays His glory by,
   Born that man no more may die,
   Born to raise the sons of earth,
   Born to give them second birth.

This music was composed by Felix Mendelssohn, a famous German composer. He was not happy when it was made into a carol, as he felt the words were unsuitable for the tune.

In the Bleak Midwinter

1. In the bleak midwinter
   Frosty wind made moan,
   Earth stood hard as iron,
   Water like a stone.
   Snow had fallen snow on snow,
   Snow on snow,
   In the bleak midwinter,
   Long ago.

2. What can I give him,
   Poor as I am?
   If I were a shepherd
   I would bring a lamb.
   If I were a wise man
   I would do my part,
   Yet what I can I give him
   Give my heart.

Gustav Holst was one of the great English composers of this century. In 1906 he was commissioned to write music for a new hymn book. This is one of his compositions for it.

Recorder 1

Recorder 2

or Recorder 3

I Saw Three Ships

1. I saw three ships come sailing in,
   On Christmas Day, on Christmas Day,
   I saw three ships come sailing in,
   On Christmas Day in the morning.

2. And what was in those ships all three?

3. Our Saviour Christ and His Ladye.

4. And all the bells on earth shall ring.

5. And all the angels in Heav'n shall sing.

The tunes of many early carols were written not only to be played and sung, but also to be danced to. This tune, with its lively rhythm, was probably meant for just that.

Recorder 1

Recorder 2

Drum

*Fifth verse only

Joy to the World

1. Joy to the world! The Lord has come,
   Let earth receive her King.
   Let every heart
   Prepare him room,
   And heav'n and nature sing,
   And heav'n and nature sing,
   And heaven, and heaven and nature sing.

2. Hark, hark, what news! What joyful news!
   To all the nations round.
   Today rejoice
   A King is born
   Who is with glory crowned,
   Who is with glory crowned,
   Who is with glory, with glory crowned.

George Frederick Handel wrote the music for this carol.
He was born in Germany in 1685.

O Christmas Tree

O Christmas tree, O Christmas tree,
How lovely are your branches.
O Christmas tree, O Christmas tree,
How lovely are your branches.
In beauty green they'll always grow
Through summer sun and winter snow.
O Christmas tree, O Christmas tree,
How lovely are your branches.

The words of this carol are from Germany, and are traditional.

O Come, All Ye Faithful

1. O come, all ye faithful,
   Joyful and triumphant,
   O come ye, O come ye to Bethlehem.
   Come and behold Him,
   Born the King of Angels,
   O come, let us adore Him,
   O come, let us adore Him,
   O come, let us adore Him, Christ the Lord.

2. See how the shepherds,
   Summoned to His cradle,
   Leaving their flocks, draw nigh to gaze.
   We too will thither
   Bend our joyful footsteps.

3. Sing, choirs of angels,
   Sing in exultation,
   Sing, all ye citizens of heaven above.
   Glory to God
   In the highest.

The original words for this carol were in Latin -
"Adeste Fideles". The melody is English, and can be
traced back over two hundred years.

Recorder 1

Recorder 2

*First verse only

19

O Come, O Come, Emmanuel

1. O come, O come, Emmanuel,
   Redeem thy captive Israel
   That mourns in lonely exile here,
   Until the Son of God appear.
   Rejoice! Rejoice! Emmanuel
   Shall come to thee, O Israel.

2. O come, O come, thou Lord of Might,
   Who to thy tribes, on Sinai's height
   In ancient times didst give the law
   In cloud, and majesty, and awe.

3. O come, thou Key of David, come,
   And open wide our heavenly home.
   Make safe the way that leads on high,
   And close the path to misery.

In the Hebrew language, the word for "God" is considered too holy to say. "El" is one of several words that are used instead. "Emmanuel" means "God is with us".

Recorder 1

Recorder 2

Recorder 3

21

O Little Town of Bethlehem

1. O little town of Bethlehem,
   How still we see thee lie.
   Above thy deep and dreamless sleep
   The silent stars go by.
   Yet in thy dark streets shineth
   The everlasting light.
   The hopes and fears of all the years
   Are met in thee tonight.

2. O morning stars, together
   Proclaim the holy birth,
   And praises sing to God the King,
   And peace to men on earth.
   For Christ is born of Mary,
   And, gathered all above,
   While mortals sleep, the angels keep
   Their watch of wondering love.

3. How silently, how silently
   The wondrous gift is given.
   So God imparts to human hearts
   The blessings of his heaven.
   No ear may hear his coming,
   But in this world of sin,
   Where meek souls will receive him, still
   The dear Christ enters in.

The tune of this carol is English, and was handed
down through several centuries. The famous English
composer, Vaughan Williams, wrote it down and
arranged it, using words that were written by an
American, Bishop Phillips Brooks.

Recorder 1

Recorder 2

Once in Royal David's City

1. Once in royal David's city
   Stood a lowly cattle shed,
   Where a mother laid her baby
   In a manger for his bed.
   Mary was that mother mild,
   Jesus Christ her little child.

2. He came down to earth from heaven,
   Who is God and Lord of all,
   And his shelter was a stable,
   And his cradle was a stall.
   With the poor and mean and lowly,
   Lived on earth our Saviour holy.

3. And through all his wondrous childhood
   He would honour and obey,
   Love and watch the lowly maiden
   In whose gentle arms he lay.
   Christian children all must be
   Mild, obedient, good as he.

4. And our eyes at last shall see him,
   Through his own redeeming love,
   For that child so dear and gentle
   Is our Lord in heav'n above.
   And he leads his children on
   To the place where he is gone.

The words of this carol were written by Mrs C. F. Alexander. She was the wife of Archbishop Alexander, head of the Church of Ireland.

Recorder 1

Tuned Percussion
or Recorder 2

On Christmas Night

1. On Christmas night all Christians sing,
   To hear the news the angels bring.
   On Christmas night all Christians sing,
   To hear the news the angels bring.
   News of great joy, news of great mirth,
   News of our merciful King's birth.

2. Then why should men on earth be so sad,
   Since our Redeemer made us glad?
   When from our sin he sets us free,
   All for to gain our liberty.

3. All out of darkness we have light,
   Which made the angels sing this night:
   "Glory to God, and peace to men,
   Now and for evermore. Amen."

This is another of the many old English carols that were
also dances. It was written down by Vaughan Williams.

Past Three O'Clock

Past three o' clock,
And a cold and frosty morning,
Past three o' clock,
Good morrow masters all.

1. Born is a baby, gentle as may be,
   Son of th'eternal Father supernal.

2. Seraph choir singeth, angel bell ringeth,
   Hark how they rhyme it, time it and chime it.

3. Light out of star-land leadeth from far land.
   Princes, to meet him, worship and greet him.

This carol was written by Charles Wood. He was born
about a hundred years ago in Ireland, and moved to
London where he became a music teacher.

Rocking

1. Little Jesus, sweetly sleep, do not stir,
   We will lend a coat of fur.
   We will rock you, rock you, rock you,
   We will rock you, rock you, rock you.
   See the fur to keep you warm,
   Snugly round your tiny form.

2. Mary's little baby, sleep, sweetly sleep,
   Sleep in comfort, slumber deep.
   We will rock you, rock you, rock you,
   We will rock you, rock you, rock you.
   We will serve you all we can,
   Darling, darling little man.

The melody of this carol is a folk tune from
Czechoslovakia. It is a lullaby.

Silent Night

1. Silent night, holy night,
   All is calm, all is bright.
   Round yon virgin mother and child,
   Holy infant, so tender and mild.
   Sleep in heavenly peace.
   Sleep in heavenly peace.

2. Silent night, holy night,
   Shepherds, hushed, saw the light.
   Glories stream from heaven afar.
   Heav'nly hosts sing Alleluia!
   Christ the Saviour is here.
   Christ the Saviour is here.

In the year 1818, just before Christmas, in a small
Austrian village, there was a problem - the church
organ broke down. So the priest and a local
schoolmaster together wrote this carol, to be sung
simply and without any organ accompaniment.

Recorder 1

Recorder 2

Tuned Percussion
or Recorder 3

The First Nowell

1. The first Nowell the angel did say
Was to certain poor shepherds in fields as they lay.
In fields where they lay, keeping their sheep,
On a cold winter's night that was so deep.

Nowell, Nowell, Nowell, Nowell,
Born is the King of Israel.

2. They lookèd up and saw a star
Shining in the east, beyond them far,
And to the earth it gave great light,
And so it continued both day and night.

3. And by the light of that same star,
Three Wise Men came from country far.
To seek for a King was their intent,
And to follow the star wherever it went.

"Nowell", meaning Christmas, is a Norman word. It
has been in the English language for a thousand years.

Recorder 1

Recorder 2

Tuned Percussion
or Recorder 3

35

The Holly and the Ivy

1. The holly and the ivy,
   When they are both full grown,
   Of all the trees that are in the wood,
   The holly bears the crown.

   O the rising of the sun
   And the running of the deer,
   The playing of the merry organ
   Sweet singing in the choir.

2. The holly bears a blossom
   White as the lily flower,
   And Mary bore sweet Jesus Christ
   To be our sweet Saviour.

3. The holly bears a berry
   As red as any blood
   And Mary bore sweet Jesus Christ,
   To do poor sinners good.

This is a very old English folk song, probably originating
in the fourteenth century. It was collected at the
beginning of this century by Cecil Sharp.

Recorder

Tambourine

*First verse only

Tyrolean Cradle Song

1. The shadows are falling, the evening's at hand.
   To watch by thy cradle, my Saviour, I stand.
   A song I am singing, to lull Thee to sleep,
   O rest now from crying, safeguard will I keep.
   O sleep, O rest, Thou sweetest and best.

2. Forget for a moment the sorrows of earth,
   Man's burden of sin that Thou bearest from birth.
   Forget the poor stable where Thou must rest,
   If Thou dost accept it, no palace so blest.
   O sleep, O rest, Thou sweetest and best.

This carol is a lullaby. The Tyrolean mountains are part of the Alps.

Recorder 1

Recorder 2

Tuned Percussion
or Recorder 3

*First verse

Unto Us a Boy is Born

1. Unto us a boy is born,
   King of all creation,
   Come He to a world forlorn,
   The Lord of every nation.

2. Cradled in a stall was He,
   With sleepy cows and asses.
   But the very beasts could see
   That He all men surpasses.

3. Herod then with fear was filled,
   "A prince," he said, "In Jewry!"
   All the little boys he killed
   At Bethl'em in his fury.

4. Now may Mary's Son, who came
   So long ago to love us,
   Lead us all with hearts aflame
   Unto the joys above us.

Here is another carol that was originally in Latin –
"Puer Nobis Nascitur". It can be traced back five
hundred years ago to Germany.

Recorder 1

Recorder 2

*The slur refers only to the word setting.

We Three Kings

1. We three Kings of Orient are,
   Bearing gifts we traverse afar
   Field and fountain, moor and mountain,
   Following yonder star.

   O star of wonder, star of night,
   Star with royal beauty bright.
   Westward leading, still proceeding,
   Guide us to thy perfect light.

2. Glorious now behold him arise,
   King and God and sacrifice.
   Heav'n sings "Alleluia",
   "Alleluia" the earth replies.

This carol was written by an American, the Reverend
Dr. Hopkins of Pennsylvania.

We Wish You a Merry Christmas

1. We wish you a merry Christmas,
   We wish you a merry Christmas,
   We wish you a merry Christmas,
   And a happy New Year.

   Glad tidings we bring
   To you and your kin,
   We wish you a merry Christmas
   And a happy New Year.

2. Now bring us some figgy pudding,
   And bring some out here.

3. For we all like figgy pudding,
   So bring some out here.

4. And we won't go until we've got some,
   So bring some out here.

This secular carol is from the West Country, England.

44

Recorder 1

Tuned Percussion
or Recorder 2

Maracas

*Third and fourth
verses only

While Shepherds Watched

1. While shepherds watched their flocks by night,
   All seated on the ground,
   The angel of the Lord came down,
   And glory shone around.

2. "Fear not," said he, for mighty dread
   Had seized their troubled mind.
   "Glad tidings of great joy I bring
   To you and all mankind."

3. "To you in David's town this day
   Is born of David's line
   A Saviour who is Christ the Lord,
   And this shall be the sign:"

4. "The heavenly babe you there shall find
   To human view displayed,
   All meanly wrapped in swathing bands
   And in a manger laid."

This is an old English folk-melody which an Irishman, Nahum Tate, heard about three hundred years ago. He added the verses, using the words of St. Luke in the Bible.

Acknowledgements

The publishers with to thank the following who have kindly given permission for the use of copyright material: Oxford University Press for permission to use the music 'Cranham' by Gustav Holst (1874-1934) from the *English Hymnal* and for permission to reproduce the carol 'Rocking' from the *Oxford Book of Carols*.